MY JOURNEY
to Freedom

*Making the choice to
rebuild my life after sexual abuse*

an account by
SATERRIA SPRINGER NORAH

MY JOURNEY TO FREEDOM

Published by Atiya's Light Publishing
A Division of Ingram & Atiya Enterprises, LLC
United States of America

Edited by Le Shaundra Muhammad

Atiya's Light Publishing
www.atiyaslight.com
info@atiyaslight.com

Library of Congress Control Number: 2015936198
ISBN: 978-0-9916444-7-6

Printed in the United States of America

For my husband and our children; my parents, Charles and Peggy Springer;

my brothers Gary Moore, Omar Moore and Charles Springer III; and finally

for the many people struggling to find their healing. God is not through with

us yet.

Acknowledgements

Giving thanks to Almighty God for guiding me and keeping me, I'm forever thankful.

Thanks to my husband who never allowed me to give up. I can hear him now saying, "Did you work on your book today? If you just start it, the words will flow." Thank you for not allowing me to give up. I kept your words in my head when I felt that I could not do it. Thank you Roscoe, I love you so much!

Thanks to my children for being patient. You are bright stars. Continue to let your light shine.

Thanks to my mother who kept late nights with me listening to all the ideas I had for this book, that book, and many other books. It means much to know that you believe in me and was willing to not only help plan a book signing even before there was a book, but for investing in me and my dream. Thank you mother, I love and appreciate you.

Thanks to my friend Victor Muhammad. He has always kept it real and introduced me to some of the best people I know.

Thanks to the team at Atiya's Light Publishing Company. You were able to see beyond my pain and into my heart to help me stand in my truth. Thank you for not allowing me to hide behind the many veils and for pushing me to express my real self.

Thanks to the many wonderful people who have crossed my path, you too have helped this book to become a reality. To the mockers, the naysayers, and the robbers of the light of God, I thank you as well, because I know now that you can be overcome! Thank Almighty God!

Words From the Author...

Each event, circumstance, good time and bad time serves as a piece to the puzzle of life. Those pieces somehow help to bring it all together. The whole puzzle is not just made up of only difficult times or only the good times. It's a collective picture that's formed from the many experiences we go through in life. Sometimes though, we get lost in the individual events and in other people's views of us. But when we can step into our season and become who we really are, now that's a miracle.

It was several pieces of my life that lead up to the writing of this book. I pulled all the pieces out, or at least all the ones I could find, and I started to put the puzzle of my life together, one piece at a time, even those childhood pieces that I put in a box, and until now refused to take out.

I have always had a desire to write. I kept journals and records of my activities at school each day, who I talked to on the telephone, which people I liked and who I didn't like… the list goes on and on. The desire to write was always there tucked away in my heart. I discontinued writing when I stopped valuing myself. Instead, I paid more attention to other people's idea of me and that became my veil.

For years I tried to be everything and everyone else but me. I hid behind the excuses that I was not good enough and was not good at writing because English, spelling, and grammar was not my greatest strength. I kept up the excuses because it was easier than facing and overcoming the challenges. It was easier being someone else, because being me was too much work. But, no matter how hard I tried to get away from myself, reality confronted me daily and to get through the pain, I was forced to write.

One day, after coming home feeling rejected and like there was no place else to go, I sat down in front of my computer with tears rolling down my face. Nothing seemed to be going right. Writing a book was the last thing on my mind at that moment. As I started to write, one sentence led to another, and before I knew it there were many pages in front of me. I felt like this information needed to be shared, and that somehow by doing so, a healing could take place not only in my life, but possible in someone else's life as well.

I approached a friend and requested to speak to the people in their congregation. That door was not open for me to share. So, when I went to get my hair done, I asked the hairdresser if he mind listening to what I wrote. He said yes, and after he heard the words that were written, he insisted that the information needed to be shared with others. That writing was called, "Feminine Energy" and with those four pages, I began writing my first book.

People desire to be free. They desire to be released from bondage whether it is financial, negativity, imposed traditions, expectations, imagery, or whatever. They want freedom, and more than anything else, I wanted freedom too. I wanted to be free of the need to be validated by others. I wanted to be free of the false sense of self. I wanted to be free from feeling the need to ask for permission to live my life as myself. What I realized is that my journey to freedom started with the pen. It started that very day at the computer when I found the courage to begin writing my thoughts and feelings down.

This book evolved out of a process of me learning to accept myself regardless of my flaws or weaknesses. It became the road to emotional healing. I learned that the journey to real freedom starts internally and no matter how much I looked outside of myself or blamed others for what was wrong in my life, the real person keeping me locked up was me. The real person keeping me held in captivity was me. I discovered that the majority of what kept me bound is only an illusion, an image that I had created in my own mind.

Sure there are things in life that exists, and circumstances that may become stumbling blocks, but when you choose to live your life without the masks and step from behind the veil of others, you experience something pretty amazing.

I wrote this book first to get out what I was feeling and then to provide insight on the importance of valuing yourself and not to let others define who you are. As you read it, I can only hope and pray that you get the message I am seeking, in my own special way, to impart. Insight can give a person valuable "outsight." Often we look outside of ourselves, when the answers are usually within. The Creator has given us everything we need.

The focus of this book was women because as women we have a huge amount of influence on the world around us. We are the mothers of our civilization. We are the teachers of the children. I wanted women to understand that when we find ourselves and live in the nature of who we really are, we bring balance to our universe and harmony to our families. When we as women can step from behind the many veils we hide behind and deal with the hurt and pain and overcome the ego, we will stop perpetuating the abuse that society has rendered unto the female for generations. The greatest justice we as women can deliver to the world is to stand in our divine feminine energy.

The longing for freedom is what motivated me to start writing again and now to keep writing. I longed for personal freedom for far too long and if this book which charts my own journey to freedom can help others to break free from the prison that locks them in, praise God!

Freedom is defined as "the power or right to act, speak, or think as one wants without hindrance or restraint."

There are many people out there who face the same struggle as I did – Self-identity. Like I was, you might be one of those people who are blind to yourself and as a result have no idea as to where you are going in life. You might be deaf to the voice within that speaks the truth or you may try to drown it out by the flood of other people's ideas about who you.

I allowed myself to be hindered by a false sense of self. I wore masks to be accepted and fashioned myself from the clay of rejection, fear, and pain. I lived my present standing in my past all the while trying to find a way to experience my true rhythm. But, I came to the realization that our "flow" is produced by being authentic and by accepting the gift of who we are that the Creator created us to be.

So this journey has brought about a peace that was not there before now. Vanity had to go, and so did fear. Instead, I began trusting God to do the guiding. I stepped out on faith. I challenged pain, humiliation, self-doubt and fear of rejection. I started believing in myself again, and by believing in me more, I got to know myself better, and in getting to know me, I found direct connection to God.

Writing this book is actively participating in my healing and in creating the story of my life. I am a unique star that shines brightly. I do not have to give my power away to shine or borrow someone else's light. While I may not be able to change the past, I can shape the present. I intend to continue on my journey to freedom because my destiny awaits and in the process help others along the way!

Table of Contents

Introduction...

If it were not for the broken pieces, I would have never looked deep into my soul to find the truth of my heart. It wasn't until I started listening to the voice within and trusting that voice that I began to realize I was finally being led on a road to finding freedom, joy, and inner-peace . I made the choice to no longer allow fear to get in my way. I wanted to live. Therefore, I had to come out, somehow, someway. I heard a voice say, "Be yourself and step out on what you already know is true." So, I started re-claiming myself.

I was no longer willing to wait for the perfect moment. I decided to make the moment perfect for me. I picked myself up because I was now on a journey that I had been looking for. The thing is, it was already a part of me and as I reflected back through the years, I cried rivers of tears. That cooled my soul giving me strength to carry on. As I reflected, I saw the mountain of troubles that kept me climbing higher. And you know what? When you overcome the pain of the struggle of getting over that mountain, you actually can see a beautiful view. At a certain point of me climbing, I finally looked at myself and said, "The journey to freedom is in me."

I was now aware of my surroundings and I noticed from listening to my inner voice that I was in the classroom of self-mastery; and all of the lesson plans were made especially to fit me. There was nowhere to hide. I could choose to keep running, repeating the same 'ole trials by trying to be someone else or I could set out for the promise land, which was founded in the truth of my heart. I no longer wanted to replay the "Imitation of Life." I realized the views that I had developed of myself were based on what others have said of me; and what they said was far from true. The greatest lesson that I am learning on this journey, is to embrace who I am and to accept my own unique gifts because by sharing my gifts I can be of a greater service to the world.

The feeling of picking up one piece of the internal puzzle and self-connecting it to another piece felt so empowering. With the connection of each, I felt more alive and more connected with the world around me. I could feel life in the wind as it blew. Each time I took a step, I felt the energy illuminating from the ground. Every breath I took, I felt life enter. I couldn't go back to false service to others by trying to gain their approval. The impact of becoming me was so strong and life-giving.

Because I wanted to live, the same way I go through the process of breathing by inhaling and exhaling, I started to do it with my life experiences. Breathing in and then out. I inhale the lessons of life that's wrapped as beautiful gifts; and I exhale the beauty to others. Every time we share our story, the light of understanding is made brighter for someone else and as they pass it on the light becomes brighter and before we know it path becomes well-lit.

1
GATHERING THE SCATTERED PIECES

Picking up parts of self you thought didn't exist,
the same pieces that others resist.
Putting yourself together again, molding in truth:
telling your story and putting your life to use.
Building up what they perceived as down,
and sitting yourself upon solid ground.
Your identity is clear;
and your kingdom is here.
Bow to the Creator; accept your crown.
It's your time and that time is now!

You are now at a point within your life where you are ready to let it all go! You are ready to become free of your false reality. No longer do you wish to define yourself by your accomplishments, your job, your beauty, your car, house or relationships. You are starting to see that these things are not the true definition of life.

I remember being at this point. It seemed like nothing really mattered anymore. Nothing that I was doing was really pleasing to my soul. Jobs that I thought I wanted had become a burden. Even being a parent had become a burden. My marriage, my faith in God, it all had become a burden. I did not understand why because I knew I loved God, my husband, my children and I loved the accomplishments that I had made but it just did not feel like I was being true to myself. There was a deep desire in my soul to be myself. My purpose in life had to be more than surviving.

Was I to go to school to get an education so that I could be qualified to work a better paying job, and then use that money from the better paying job to pay for the necessities of life? Was it really only about food, clothing, and shelter? Was I to do that day in and day out until I reached a level of retirement or death? No! This could not be my purpose in life. I thought to myself, "Is it only about being a mother, wife, sister, niece, aunt, cousin or friend?"

I was now starting to recognize that something had happened to me.

Confusion, doubt, uncertainty and fear started to kick in. I was unsure about my real feelings. The truth is sometimes hard to see, let alone accept when you are constantly trying to validate yourself by other people's standard. There is a constant battle between the false you and the real you. And the truth keeps trying to push its way out, and the more that happens, the more that falsehood is being exposed. At that point you are confronted with a choice. I had to finally choose whether I wanted to continue to live a lie, wearing the many masks I had picked up along the way, or was I really ready to start living as me.

"Two things cannot occupy the same space at the same time."

You're going to be real or fake, hot or cold, right or wrong, good or bad, but you cannot be both at the same time. You have to make a choice.

I asked myself, "Do you, Saterria want to choose to stay inside an un-fulfilled life surrounded by vanity, guilt and fear; or do you face the reality of your situation and go to war with falsehood to change it?"

I chose freedom. I wanted to be myself - my true self, and that to me is real freedom. I was no longer willing to hide behind the veil of darkness or in the shadows of others. I wanted my light to shine too. I was not who I was claiming to be. That was only a façade. So, when I found myself at a cross roads, I knew it was decision-making time. And the hardest part of it all, at that moment, was to believe in myself.

The voice within me said, "You're great and God sent you here to fulfill a higher calling."

The more I listened to the internal voice, the louder it became and I was able to receive new direction.

"How did I get this way?"

"How long have I been this way?"

A flood of questions came to me, and so did answers. I wanted to know. But in order to know, I had to face the truth. I had to stop hiding from it.

Growing up, I experienced major events that caused a lot of pain and hurt. I carried this pain through life. I know that I am not the only one who has experienced pain in life.

Many people have been the victims of verbal, mental, physical, and/or sexual abuse - sometimes at the very hands of our own loved ones and family members. Some have also inflicted pain on themselves and the people around them.

I perpetuated the pain in my life in many ways, and in my denial of the truth, I projected that pain onto others. But when you make the decision to be real with your life and stop faking or hiding behind others you own what's yours.

I can remember being caught up in this circle of pain. It started for me like this:

In my family, there were six of us - my parents, my three brothers and me. As far as the children were concerned, I was the only girl and also the youngest. Growing up wasn't all bad though. My mother made me feel loved. There was no doubt that I felt the warmth coming from her heart. She had a way of making all of her children feel loved.

Being the only daughter and the youngest too, it was sometimes like being the only person or thing in the world. Even though she had many things to accomplish in a day, I never felt like I was not getting the attention needed. From her cosmetology work, keeping the house clean, cooking and being a mother and wife she still made time to show love to us individually in our own way. My mother made sure our home stayed cleaned I recall how when she would clean, she played the best music. She played songs by Tina Turner, Whitney Houston, High Five, Janet Jackson and others. I loved those times because I could sing along with the music she played.

My mother prepared home-cooked meals every night. Yes, he was our mother, but she was also a mother to the community. My brothers' friends were at our house every day. The girls from up the street and around the corner were always at our house and my mother treated them just like they were her very own children. My father was my personal hero. I can remember one day my daddy built a beautiful back porch patio just for me. It had a set of small wooden chairs and the matching table. It was beautiful. I sat out on this back patio many of days playing school because I wanted to be a teacher. My cousins played school with me. They were the pupils and they allowed me to be the teacher.

My daddy often stopped by the house during his lunch break with his coworker who would give me peppermints. During the afternoons, our home would be rocking with warmth, music and love! The smell of food, the feeling of love and the sound of the lead and bass guitar, the drums, the keyboard and all the voices from my dad's gospel group called the Heavenly Host was amazing. After I graduated from head start, my daddy would always sing the graduation song to me that we sang at our head start graduation.

"Over here, over there,
there's some head start children
that will be in public school next year…"

Back then I was my true self. My self-esteem was high and I didn't have the challenges of expressing myself. I was happy and it was great to be me. I felt free, protected, and loved for a little while anyway. But things started to change.

As time went on, I began to notice things that I hadn't noticed before. Police started coming to our home. My mother's belongings would get thrown out in the streets. Our home would be trashed. I witnessed my mother's face bleeding and constant fighting from my parent's room.

The abuse happening in my home quickly became my new reality. Things became so bad that I became afraid to live at home. One night my dad started really hurting my mother and so I ran across the street to my grandmother's house lived for her to call the police. Even now I can recall how I felt. I became afraid and started to doubt things.

My mother soon after that incident moved out and we got our own place. My daddy would come by our new place to pick me up. Frequently he sent letters to my mother through me. I don't know what was in those letters, but before I knew it, we were moving back into our home with my dad.

The night of the move, I was in my room with my brother's girlfriend. My cousin stormed into the room yelling.

"Omar just got killed!"

I was stunned. Although I was only about six years old, I did understand that I would never see my brother again. Omar left the house that day and never made it back home again. He was riding his moped on his way back home when he was killed. A friend was chasing him down Marstellar Street in Wilmington, North Carolina when he was hit by a truck. It was a week before his 16th birthday. I watched my mother die internally hearing the news. My Grandmother screamed at the top of her lungs.

"Omar!"

Things were never the same in our home after that. What was a warm and loving home, turned cold and lonely.

It wasn't too long after that, when my parents divorced. I came home from school one day to see my daddy sitting on the bottom of the steps crying. It was the first time I had seen a man cry. But it wasn't just any man, it was my daddy! Everything was already moved out of my room. I was confused. Everything that was familiar seemed like it was gone. It seemed to all happen overnight.

My mother, older brother, and I moved in with my grandmother in the country until we were able to get our own place. I missed my family and friends. I did not like the people my parents had become! My other brother stayed with my dad, while I started a new school with new people, and a new area. Things just weren't going good for me. I started struggling in school. I flunked second grade. I became a bully, and stayed in trouble. I developed a reputation for being a trouble maker and that is exactly how people started to deal with me. On top of that I got fat! I gained so much weight that I was teased by family members and others. The happy Saterria became depressed, out of control and food became her comfort.

Dealing with my father abusing my mother, my parents divorcing, and my brother's death was very hard for me. I was very young and while I do not know all the details of everything that happened, what I do remember was the pain of it all. I could not imagine things getting any worse, but they did and something very tragic happened.

When I was about seven years old my uncle hurt me. He started molesting me. By the time I was eight years of age, I tried to tell, but nobody believed me. Instead, I was called a liar. I had nowhere to run to and nowhere to hide so I internalized all that hurt that was surrounding me and became what others said of me. My daddy stopped being my hero and my mother stopped being the loving, kind-hearted queen in my eyes. I didn't like them anymore!

I began living out of fear, hate, doubt and low self-esteem, and I treated others based on how I was feeling about myself. I blamed my parents because they got a divorce. I blamed them for almost everything and my relationship with them was no longer genuine.

I was slowly becoming someone else. I put on a false persona as my way of coping with the pain of being robbed of my innocence. I pretended it didn't happen and did my best to not talk about it. I overcompensated by acting tough and strong when honestly I felt like a trapped, scared little girl.

The fear became the engine of my life and I held on to poisonous relationships. How could I really love the people around me when I didn't even love myself? How could I love myself when I wasn't even being myself? How could I be myself when I didn't even know who I was separate from all the bottled up pain inside? Much happened to me and around me as a little girl that I grew up running from the truth. I didn't lie about my uncle molesting me, but after a while, I did start to lie about who I was.

I didn't own up to the feelings of shame and the self-hate that being molested caused me. I hid behind a false reality telling myself all the years of my life that it did not bother me when it did. It changed how I viewed myself and my family. I thought God hated me. How could the Creator allow me to be abused in a way like that? I was a helpless child! I was hurt by someone I trusted by someone my and who my parents trusted.

The pain of it ran very deep. But I grew up acting like it didn't bother me. There were many visible side-effects and as a way to cope with what I was feeling inside, I masked it by self-medicating. I started smoking marijuana and drinking alcohol. I didn't go to God because I felt like He allowed me to be molested. I wouldn't go to any other family members because most of them didn't believe I was telling the truth. I hated them and I hated myself.

I felt ugly and ashamed and for years, I kept all those feelings bottled up inside. My relationships ended in pain and I continued to draw painful experiences into my life. I knew that love was truth, but I was living a lie. I was in bondage. I was a broken little girl who grew up to be a broken woman – emotionally, mentally, and spiritually.

I was vulnerable and broken by circumstances, hurt, and pain and those broken pieces became scattered by the winds of life. Each time the wind blew, a piece of me went with it blowing in different directions. Each place that the broken me landed, became the place where I pick up new identities. I became what others said I was or what they said

I should be. Their truth became mine. My teachers said I was a problem child. At home I was labeled the instigator. My peers called me a bully and a troublemaker. And you know what? I believed them. I believed every last one of them. But the truth is, I had no clue of who I was and the people around me were just as clueless. I was lost. So the more winds that blew in my life, the more scattered I became and the more my life was in pieces.

I knew deep down inside it wasn't me. But it was just too overwhelming to deal with. It was much easier hiding and pretending like everything was okay with me and the problem was everyone else. Pretending and hiding behind a veil is just too heavy of a burden to carry. When you do this, it causes you to hide your own gifts and talents.

Your gifts are supposed to be shared with the world. Sharing your gifts helps others in their true service to God. The desire to write, teach and sing was like an alarm clock in my head awakening me to the real me. God was calling me through what was already in me, I just had to first stop hiding behind all of these other people and their personas, accept me for me, and then start to gather all the scattered pieces. The next step was for me to just start being me.

My Aha Moment:

In life we sometimes allow people and circumstances to separate us from our true self. When this happens, it disconnects us from the Creator. God is the connector of everything in the universe. Each time we are faced with a difficult moment in our life that we don't confront, we start to break down instead of being built up.

If you are not rooted in yourself, the breakdown can leave your life in pieces, and those pieces can sometimes become scattered during the storms of life.

Between the ages of five and eight, I witnessed my father abusing my mother, my brother died, my parents divorced, and I was molested. My life was just starting out during the times of building a strong foundation. But circumstances changed things and as a result my life was in scattered pieces.

As I began gathering the scattered pieces of my life, I learned that every part of me matters and is worth putting back together. Even those parts I don't understand or agree with, they are still important.

I learned that my true identity is wrapped up in every piece of me and that I can use what was broken as a bridge to understanding me. I learned that I can become an architect of my own life, designing each part according to what's true for me.

The vision of Saterria became clearer and sharpened in the process of gathering all of my scattered pieces in that it taught me to see beyond the problem to discovering the solution.

The Journey...

Digging deep into the seas of your mind;
unraveling your truth and living in real time.
Exploring your thoughts and in return creating ideas;
living in your truth and working out Gods will.
You are already apart of the plan;
no need to recreate what's already in your hand.

Use your tool and build your life;
drop the idols and self-made pride.
Those are the things you use to hide;
but it's time to come out now.
Claim your God giving right;
the battle on the outside is over.

Win your internal fight.
Stand up in your truth;
and use God's word as your proof.
Lift your head up high.
There is no limit when you know
how to navigate the sky.

The Journey is yours, claim it and be.
Your truth is waiting to set you free.
The Creator's promises are real,
align yourself up with His will.

And soon you will see
that you play a major role
in renewing a world that has been made so cold.
Warm it up with your light.
It's your time.
Always shine bright.

2
Rising Above Hurt and pain

Step into a new reality and recreate the view
Know that the pain doesn't define you.
Elevate, be concise, and change the altitude.
Glide above the seas;
become one with the breeze.
Success you once perceived as stress?
Look into the mirror and see your best.
You've already passed half the test.
So, make history, because you're writing the rest.

To rise is to move from a lower position to a higher one. After finally recognizing and accepting the fact that I had been living in a cycle of pain, it was time to step up. So, I made a choice. Rising above the hurt came to me in steps. I didn't realize it until I started thinking over my life. I had to be strong enough to just let it all go. Let the hurt go. Let the pain go. Let the blaming go and deal with myself.

At first, I found myself fighting old thought patterns. As soon as the negative thoughts came up I commanded those thoughts to leave. Each time I did this, I became stronger and stronger. I listened to my inner voice and kicked all of those other voices out of my head.

"You're a liar!"

"You're a trouble-maker."

"You're this or you're that…"

I treated my mind like a temple. The more I focused on getting me right, the more I started to elevate.

The life of pain I had been living was in contradiction to my original self. I believed I was created in love, peace, and happiness; but I got caught up in the pain of what happened to me and there I got stuck. For years I refused to deal with my pain. I started talking about what happened to me but indirectly so that I could be comfortable with myself. Whenever I brought up the subject of abuse, I would start my sentences off with "at least 70 percent of women were raped or molested…"

When I decided to come clean with the truth, I had to acknowledge that being a victim of molestation was a very big part of my issue. It wasn't enough for me to just talk about it, I had to do something. The something I had to do first was:

1.   Be understanding.
2.   Forgive myself.
3.   Develop a relationship with God.
4.   Go back and help heal that little girl.

I had to understand that what happened to me was not my fault. I also had to understand that there were many circumstances and factors surrounding the situation that I personally would have to confront and be honest about. It was time for me to forgive God, my parents, my uncle, my teachers, my brother and his friend, and everyone else who I felt had let me down. But most of all, I had to forgive myself. As I learned to forgive, a relationship with God started to develop. That relationship was a huge part of my awakening, it also became a pathway for me to be able to go back and begin healing that little girl who has been crying out for help for so long.

Once I made the decision to rise above the hurt and the pain and brought God into it, there was no more running from it. That is when I joined the Nation of Islam. It was in July of 2008 when my brother had the book, *Message to the Blackman*. He told me to read it, but at first I wasn't interested. It wasn't until months later when my brother's friend asked me to return the book back to my brother who had loaned it to him to read. I didn't immediately give the book back to my brother; I took the time to read it at that time.

Reading *Message to the Blackman* answered so many questions that I have had for a long time. There were things in the book that I didn't understand, so I prayed about it, and then about a week later one of my uncles came by my house and invited me to a Wednesday night meeting. Initially, I told him next time, but then as I started to walk away from him, something inside me told me to go.

When I went to the meeting with my uncle, I noticed that they were studying the same book that I had read. I thought it was a new book, but I found out that it was not. I felt the meeting that Wednesday night was very informative, so I went to the following Sunday meeting. Brother Nuri Muhammad was speaking and when I heard him speak I knew in my heart that what he was saying was right, so when they opened the doors for people to join, I joined the Nation of Islam right there in Wilmington, North Carolina!

As I studied the teachings of the Honorable Elijah Muhammad, I learned a lot and they played a very big part of my healing. They are beautiful teachings and when I joined I knew there was no doubt that I would be okay. I was ready to work on me, and that is what I did – started working on me. This journey has been very hard, because the old Saterria sometimes creeps up.

I came to the Nation with all of me including the pain and hurt too. Through the years of being in the Nation, yes there have been some good times, but mostly what I ran into was more hurt and pain. So now I had to deal with the issues I came with, and try to cope with the new issues that came along with being a member of the Nation.

I was on a journey to be free from all that was holding me back, and I expected to get saved when I walked into those doors and said yes to join because everything I was reading and studying was true for me. But instead, over the course of the years, I felt more abused and rejected. Yes, I came with all my issues, but I expected to be accepted and embraced because that is what the Most Honorable Elijah Muhammad taught.

When I joined, I was expecting to be embraced and accepted for me. I wanted healing. I wanted to be better. I followed orders, but I knew that it was more to it than just letting people control me and hide my light. And that is how I started to feel – like I was hiding my light. I was asked to help with the Muslim Girls in Training Class (M.G.T.) when I first came, and I did, but that was not enough for me. I wanted to help in a bigger way. So I got this idea to start a women's program. The program didn't happen and many reasons were stated as to why it could not happen and because I was new and didn't really know a lot about the Nation, I accepted that. I was sometimes referred to as a baby.

Overall, I felt mistreated in the study group in Wilmington and like my gifts didn't matter or was not necessary in the "mission." When I tried to express how I was feeling, I felt like people were hiding behind their titles and since I did not have a title, then my thoughts or opinions were not needed. For the most part I didn't feel that way when I traveled to other mosques and study groups. Every now and then I would sense like I was being "looked over" in some of the laborers meetings.

I have been carrying a lot of blame and passing blame. When I wasn't blaming others, I was allowing them to blame me and taking that blame on myself even when it wasn't mine to take. I took the blame from school, from home, from the mosque...

One day a sister from the mosque met with me and said to me that I was changing and that she was not use to the new Saterria and that she has never known me to miss a mosque meeting. The truth is I was tired...tired of taking the blame in the study group. I was tired of shrinking down and carrying the blame even when I shouldn't just so someone else can feel right about their self.

I began to see what real service to God looks like and for me real service is about me allowing my own light to shine so that others can see the God in me and possibly find their own light. I started learning how to stand on my truth. I just couldn't run from the hurt and the pain any more or the fear of judgment of my past. I had to walk through that darkness and into the light. I had to be honest with myself. I had done everything but face self. So, this was it, I was going to face Saterria's pain and all the hurt she had bottled up inside of her. And you know what, behind all of those lies I found my truth.

If I were to say anything to the people who have hurt me or mocked me, this is what I would say to them:

"All of you who judge people based off of your small, corrupted and painful mindset need to step aside and let those who are striving to start the process of self-resurrection be! Some of you are worse than the slave masters hiding behind the disguise of righteousness using your poisonous mouths to poison the minds of those who wish to do Gods work! Stop acting like your titles give you a connection to God that others don't have. I've read the books and God is not a respecter of any of that! So step out of the way with your fear because

some of us are not afraid to claim the promise land. We believe the promise of God, and that victory is ours because in this book [Holy Qur'an], there is no doubt in it. So stop trying to make me doubt myself and Almighty God!"

See, I have issues from my childhood, but so do most of us. That little girl inside of me needs to be healed and I am working on that now. And I am no longer willing to allow anyone else stop me from that process. All the stuff with the study group, that is just more "stuff" to deal with. I'm not running. I'm being myself. The inability to see past my hurt and pain caused me a lot of disappointment. Disappointments happen in life, but what do you do with it? I know what I'm doing!

I stayed in my pain and hurt for years and the only way I could see my way out was to be re-birthed out of it. The hurt and pain brought to my attention an area of my life that needed healing.

There is nothing wrong with asking, "Why am I hurting?"

"Why am I in so much pain?"

It is only when you ask the questions that you find the answers.

I realized that as long as you stay on the surface level of your pain, it will keep you in a low condition of life. This just makes it easy for you to become a slave to others. As long as you're down, people can walk all over you. That's a living hell! When you stay in the same condition for too long, in my opinion you are not moving. Without motion you really have no life. So, why stay stuck in a mental hell burning yourself with the same pain that you been burning yourself with your whole life? Why not rise from the grave of hurt, be shaped by the fire of pain and created into something new?

There is a treasure within me, but I have to be willing to look for it, and that takes me looking at and within me! So what I say to myself is this…

"If you seek you will find.
Rise, Rise, Rise to your life
becoming born again in truth.
Become elevated off of life."

Before I could even make a choice I had to really look in the mirror and see myself. I had to accept the responsibility for my present condition. No longer could I blame my past. No longer could I blame my friends. No longer could I blame myself for what was not mine. The blame game had to be over!

As long as I continued to blame other people, I wouldn't feel the need to respond to the duty of creating my own happiness and being who I really am. Once I stopped blaming people and circumstances, my mind became silent for a while. It was during this silence that I was able to see that most of my previous motives were generated from other people's thoughts. I responded to what other people had put in the atmosphere.

For years most of what I had done had been generated by everything on the outside. Now it was time to make choices from within. I became uncomfortable with my surroundings. I became uncomfortable with the conversations that I was used to engaging in. Not that the conversations were low, but because my authentic self was absent in those conversations. I became uncomfortable with being fake. I just didn't feel good about being that false Saterria who wanted to be accepted by everyone and wanted to please everyone. I still loved the people around me, but I also was falling in love with myself. So, it was no longer acceptable being what other people wanted me to be.

This gave me a new perspective on love. I realized that love had nothing to do with being available to people all the time. Love had nothing to do with keeping other people comfortable. Love had nothing to do with the material world. Love was doing what it took to live the life that I was created to live, and by living this way I could properly love the people around me.

Thoughts that used to be allowed in my mind were no longer allowed. I just could not think with boundaries or doubt anymore.

Every time a thought like that came up, the voice within self said, "This is an excuse to stay the same. Eliminate that thought instantly."

After a while, it seemed like all of my thoughts were getting pushed out of my mind! I then noticed that all of the thoughts that I was carrying and allowing into my mind were keeping the false me alive and since I made the choice to be the real Saterria all of those old thoughts had to go.

At that point, I began to realize that I was in the process of rising above my hurt and pain. I started to understand the silence. I was in a cleansing process. During this time I flushed out old thought patterns and began creating new ones. My mind had become silent for many reasons; but mainly because I was pushing everybody else out of my head. After that, I realized that after I had pushed out thoughts of guilt, negativity and doubt, what was left was just me inside the quietness of my own mind.

For the first time in years I was able to be silent and listen and when I really started listening, I realized that hearing was deeper than the words that came out of our mouths but hearing also had to do with the motivation that formulated the thoughts, which produced the words. Now I could finally hear what motivated people to say what they say.

Surprisingly, after my hearing was activated as I was rising above the pain in my life, it reactivated my sight. It seemed like I was actually seeing for the first time. When I looked, at people I didn't just see their physical bodies, I saw deeper into them. I no longer judged them by what I saw with my physical eye.

I started to understand that rising above the hurt, was elevating my mind. I was becoming a new person and this is what rising above the hurt did for me. It birthed my five senses to a higher level than just the physical level of things.

My Aha Moment:

When I stopped living inside of the hurt and pain of my life, I found new life. I found the happiness that I had been thinking about and looking for. I learned that pain is not the only way to happiness and peace and that there is a difference between struggle and pain. I had conditioned my mind to think that in order to achieve success you had to have pain. But this process taught me that you don't have to wear your pain when you struggle. The struggle was healthy because it kept me in shape towards my goal. But the pain was holding me back. I learned to look at my perception of a situation from a different set of eyes, and rise above the superstitions of my own mind.

Stripping myself of false realities
that's covered in my vanities.
Striving to unlock this pain
and accept my heavenly name.
Walking in my grace,
holding my head up high so I can
see God's face.
Using my mind as a vehicle
to take me place-to-place.
The journey is not always clear,
so, I lean on God's word and allow his truth
to steer me in the direction that is right.
Just when you feel like you're at your end,
He will come like a thief in the night
guiding you to what is right.
The fight is over; all you have to do is see
that God placed a winner within you...
and within me.

3
ACCEPTING the BEST PART of SELF

What you accept becomes a part of you
so don't accept it if it's not true.
Writing your truth is a power that the God gave you;
use it wisely and work your pen.
Tell your story from the beginning to the end.
Tell your story in the way that you move;
tell your story in your attitude.
Tell your story in your deeds.
Tell your story without apologizing.
Tell your story loud and clear;
tell your story without any fear.
You are the only YOU, so, your history
relies on you!

In continuing the journey to my personal and emotional freedom, it became clearer that it was first necessary to recognize that I was not living my true self. My identity was stolen by my pain. Before I recognized this, I was at a very low level. But, as soon as I started to reckon with my own identity and acknowledge that I had not been living, I began to rise in consciousness. As I rose in consciousness I rose to another level. I began to understand that I was actually rising above the pain in my life.

I could not continue a journey to freedom stuck in the cycle of pain that I was in. There was no fighting it. I'm not saying that pain and discomfort stopped coming, but we all have a choice to either stay in the cycle of pain or get the message from it and then rise above it. I chose the latter.

I told myself, "Saterria, if you would like to continue rising out of your mental grave, you will need to accept the best part of you."

You see to *accept* is to consent to receive a thing offered. And what was being offered to me was the opportunity to accept my own truth and greatness and the chance of a lifetime to walk in it with force and power! Regardless of what anyone else says to me…I am what I think I am. So I started thinking better of myself! Many people have thoughts of being great, but don't accept them. Instead, those thoughts become fleeting thoughts that quickly goes away because of the lack of belief. The only to manifest your greatness, is to believe in yourself and believe that you are great. People kept telling me and treating me like I was nothing. In the study group, I felt because I didn't wear a title in front of my name that I wasn't worthy of greatness, and no matter how my true self would keep trying to peep out, I kept allowing it to be hammered right back down because I didn't believe in myself or my ability to manifest my greatness.

In my opinion, and yes it is important, leads to jealousy, envy, and self-hate. I know this to be true because that is what happened to me. See, I ended up settling on the worst part of myself. I didn't want to be jealous or envious of someone else. That was not the real me! So I know if you settle on the best part of yourself, you won't be jealous of others. If you live in your truth, you won't be in competition with others because at that point you realize that there is no one else on the planet like you.

The real Saterria has always been there. But like I said before, she was hiding behind the issues, the pain, the hurt, and other personas. You know how in the animal environment when an animal senses danger they play dead, but when the threat of danger is gone, they go back to life as usual? Well, that's what I did. Whenever I felt danger or pain I hid the real me. I played dead and I didn't come out. Instead, I stayed in hiding for years, until now.

It's not really that hard to accept the best part of yourself. You just have to be brave because sometimes people will say things to push you back towards your old way of thinking.

You just have to be brave enough and politely tell them, "That is not who I am today."

Some people will not like the real you or will become uncomfortable. That's because they can no longer figure you out or have control of you. But be brave anyone. When thoughts come up in your mind about the great things you want to do in life, be brave enough to believe in yourself. Start by doing something you have always wanted to do. It could be eating healthy, working on your attitude, going back to school… whatever it is, make room for it, pray on it and take steps to complete it. Don't let anyone tell you it's not a part of the mission, because you can't help anyone else until you help yourself.

Each time I accomplished a goal that I had set for myself, I felt like I was accepting the best part of me. That kept me focused on my goal and not on the negativity. I started believing in myself so much that it gave me the courage to put pain and people who are not good for me in their proper place. So now when things happen in my life that causes me grief, instead of looking at the not so good part of it, I look into it and try to see what the Creator wants me to understand. I try to see the best part of the situation, and then that is the part I go to work to settle on. The best part of any situation in my opinion causes elevation. If you're elevating, you have movement and movement means you are alive!

At this stage, it seemed like I was losing a lot of friends and support from people who supported me at first. But I realized that these people were not my friends. They were happy with me being the false Saterria. As long as I was being fake, my inner light was dimming. These people fed off of my weaknesses, which in turn fed their darkness.

Once I started to allow my light to shine, they got uncomfortable. But my light shining helped me to see who was actually around me. For these people to continue to stay around me two things would have to happen: 1). They would have to turn their inner light on; or 2). They would have to flee from around me.

I felt like I was being judged by the people who said they loved me. Did it hurt? Yes! But because I learned the principle of rising above the pain in my life and how to start forgiving, I understood that they were only judging me based off of the cycle of pain in their lives. The only way I could help them in this stage of my development, was to keep allowing my light to shine and continue being my true self.

The truth is, I felt alone. I was alone. But, when I started accepting the best part of me, I realized that the alone time was needed. So, I was okay with that. It gave me the chance to develop myself. It gave me the chance to grow.

As time went on, I started attracting people into my life who were positive and living in their truth. My connection with the Creator became stronger. I took things in my life one day at a time. I started accepting Saterria and no longer made the excuses to hide my light. I went to my computer and starting working. I created a Facebook page called Feminine Energy named after my first attempt at writing a book and guess what? The people supported me! I didn't worry about what I didn't have. I just moved on what I knew and that was the beginning of the women's program that I had wanted to do and the rediscovery movement. And now this book, My Journey to Freedom, is officially – My Real First Book!

As one of my coaches often say, "You can have a second chance to make a good first impression."

So hello world, I am Saterria! This is the Real me!

I accept myself and I am accepting the best part of myself. I love myself. I accept my greatness and I intend to walk in it! Do I think I'm better than anyone else? No, this is not about acting like I am better than other people. It's about being the best that I can be and being truthful with who I really am, healing my issues and not allowing pain and hurt to define who I am. It's about being a better me!

See, I happen to believe that being a better you will produce excellence. This is an action that helps bring a person out of hiding and allows them to open their enclosed gifts. I became more effective by settling on the best part of myself when I stopped settling on the doubt. I knew that if I wanted to be free and begin to produce good ideas that had to change.

When you settle on the best part of yourself you will be more effective in your life and your interaction with others will be better to. You also give others the chance to know the real you. Some who were fine with you before, might not like the real you, but that is something that they have to deal with and search within themselves to find out why they think the way they do.

When I started pulling from the positive hemisphere of my mind I started seeing a difference in my life. When I really started to understand what settling on the best part of myself did, a lot of the depression and sad days disappeared. I fed the positive end of the situation. I told people about the positive perspective of things and soon my outcomes became positive. The words came out of my mouth more easily. I noticed that I began to have more of a positive effect on most people who were around me.

There is no need to be sad, depressed, or submerged in guilt. For every situation there is light in it and when you find the light you will be re-birthed out of the darkness of your situation into the light of a new day. That happened for me. As I was writing this chapter in my book, my family suffered a great loss. My cousin Latasha died. When the news came, it shocked me because it was so unexpected and sudden. I just could not grip my mind around the thought that such a young beautiful soul had left us so soon.   I experienced all types of emotions. I even questioned myself a couple times. I found myself getting stuck in the pain of her death until I could no longer enjoy the beauty of the memories we shared.

I had to keep reminding myself to stay encouraged and settle on the best part. In my mind it was and it still is hard, because I felt like there was no best part to settle on with death. How could I find the best in what I did not understand? How could I rise above the pain that hit me so deep?

I questioned myself, "Is there really good in everything?"

My questions lead me to the Creator and God showed me that the only way to rise above the pain is through humility. The way to see the best part of any situation is through being humble. When I speak of humility, I'm not speaking of some type of weak emotions. Humility takes courage because you have to be selfless. You have to take your emotions out of the situation and see it for what it is. You really have to be humble enough to see through the mind of the Creator. It was finally starting to make sense to me. I could not settle on the best part of myself based on emotions because emotions change.

I had to let go and allow the Creator to guide me by the voice within. I kept saying the word humility over and over again, and as I said it, I heard the word "hue" in it so I looked it up. Hue is a color or shade (the attribute of color by virtue of which it is discernible as red, green, etc. and which is dependent on its dominant wavelength, and independent of intensity or lightness.)

All of this lead me right back to self. See, we all have our own personal energy field around us which is called aura. Your Aura is the energy that comes from you, your aura changes depending upon your thoughts and can be felt and seen by others. It has different colors. Aura exposes many things about you. I won't go into all of that here, that is something for another time and maybe another book for now, what I will say is that we are human beings. Yet, we are alive because of the energy that the Creator allows to flow through us. It is our responsibility to keep our energy clean and healthy. We are energy. Each energy center serves a particular purpose and draws in what is needed to serve its purpose. Some people have trained their minds to see aura by opening themselves up to that process.

When you are truly humble, you are allowed to see yourself for who you really are and at that point, you become open to develop the different areas of your life that needs development. But you have to be open to the process of learning and developing. You have to be open enough to receiving the truth that comes. When truth comes, it helps to create harmony. This harmony produces a rhythm and the rhythm of your flow calls circumstances and people into your life that complements you. This is why it's important to settle on the best part.

Accepting the best part of self is like a beautiful song. You create the lyrics as the wind carries you on. You feel the truth in every step you take. I believe if you open your mind and heart that those who are for you to communicate with will relate. Accepting your truth builds up a beautiful hue within yourself and energizes your entire body.

The more I let my light shine, I feel like a rainbow operating with a healthy mind, ready to continue my journey because I can see more clearly that life is more than just you or me. Our personal journeys are for everyone. I do not believe there is any other way. I have to be who I'm created to be, and in doing so, give back to creation, keeping it rotating and alive. So I will continue my journey because there is no other place worthy for me to hide.

So, instead when I need protection or a place to retreat to, the first place I'll seek is the place of God.

My Aha Moment:

When I took the time to reason with myself, I saw that I was presented with choices. Before I just took anything on myself and then blamed God. When I started looking at both sides of a situation, and then did my best to lean toward the end that worked best for me, I noticed a shift. God blessed me with a mind, so I started putting it to use by making better decisions for my own life. I decided to accept the best part of myself and the part of me that wasn't what I wanted it to be, I decided to go to work to make it better.

I learned that I have power to direct and create a happier life. I learned that I did not have to just wait on luck to happen or for someone to give me permission to be happy and fulfilled in my life. Living like this has taught me to be a thinker and it increased my communication with God.

I learned that when I run to God about both sides of a situation and ask for His guidance, it works. This has helped me to stop blaming God for my unhappiness and accept responsibility to create peace in my own life. I also learned that when I accept the best part of myself, negative energies seems to go away. In doing this, I have been experiencing more levels of peace.

Identity

I've been looking for the girl that was stole.
Looking to see who has her on hold.
I could not find anything that resembles her soul.

I started to check her so-called friends and noticed
some of my identity was hidden in them.
When they downed my ideas, I stopped my flow,
allowing them a chance to wrap my ideas up in their minds.

Like a thief in the night
they stole my birthright,
hiding me in darkness and stealing my light.

But out of the darkness of love emerged
the one that I was destined to be.
Coming strong and claiming what's mine.
They should have known;
it would only be a matter of time
before I reclaim my mind and soul.

4
Learning to live truthfully

Live up to your full potential,
exercising your mental.
Be all that you can be,
with every breath setting yourself free.
Write your name in the skies,
not living behind the lies, or
creating unnecessary cries.
Rise! Rise! Rise!
Keep your eyes on your prize,
cultivating the twinkle in your eyes.
God gave it to you!
You just have to believe that it's true.

I had done all that I could do. I began piecing my life together, rising above my emotions and learning to settle on the best part of any given situation. At first, I was just doing the above things and continuously each time something came up within my life that I perceived as negative. Then I slowly started to notice that I was using these methods to hide deeper from my calling. Yes, I started putting the pieces to the puzzle of my life together. Yes, I was now learning to rise above painful situations and see the greater picture. Yes, I was learning to accept on the best part of a situation. I learned a lot, but I was living a little.

I realized for every piece of the puzzle that I picked up, there was a part of me that I had to let die in order to give life to the new, true and better part of me. No matter what I did, I was still somehow living in the shadows. It wasn't until I began to get in alignment that I was able to get rid of the darkness of my deeds and past that had been following me.

I had to totally let go and be myself fully and truthfully. I couldn't keep being weak in my faith. It wasn't going to work trying to one minute be the new me, then the other minute slip back into old thinking and behavior patterns.

There was something still nagging at me. So, as I continue on my journey to freedom, I noticed that I wanted to hang on to what I thought were things that made me into the woman I am today.

I actually used those same words, *"I would not be who I am today if it were not for my past that had made me this way…"*

I was still allowing the past to make me and not allowing my present to renew me. I was tired! Many people I loved and admired died. In grieving, it hit me! In order for me to transform and grow to the next level in my life, something within me must die. What we perceive as death can also be new life.

So, I thought, "In order to be the healed Saterria and take on that new mindset of being healed; and the abused mindset that Saterria was carrying around with her had to be left behind."

In order to be the happy, I had to stop being miserable. So I started to give thanks to the Creator because I realized that right within the end of something is its beginning. I could not hide behind the appearance of a well put together Saterria. I had to come face-to-face with my fears and deal with them. I had to recognize that I might have periods of darkness and I may experience different seasons in my life, but during the difficult or dark times, I do not have to lose sight of who I am. It really is all good because you're renewing and rebirthing. I had to learn to love myself enough to not be afraid to let old parts of me die to give way for new beginnings in my life.

I was rising above my emotions but my intentions were questionable. Who was I really doing it for? What was I really doing it for? Is this really making me happy? A surface level happiness will not work when you are seeking real freedom. I didn't want to just act happy, I wanted to really be happy! Besides that, acting happy will only attract other acting happy people. I didn't want that either.

The universe deals in truth, so, I had to be real with how I was feeling. Ignoring them will only lead you down a road of depression. Think about it. If you ignore your feelings and emotions, what happens? What you actually do by ignoring them is add more pressure to your life. You end up creating more things to work out.

Acknowledging and examining your emotions and feelings is necessary. In order for me to live truthfully, I had to examine myself for real. I had to deal with every aspect of myself and work at fixing my thinking. You cannot live in two worlds. You can try. I tried to live being two people, the fake me and the real me, and I can tell you, it does not work! Like I said before, I was trying to hang on to the old me and the new me at the same time. It doesn't work! It creates confusion in your thinking. It did not take me long to figure that out. You can't cover up how you feel or how others make you feel. You have to acknowledge it in order to keep elevating.

The more honest I am with myself and others about how I am feeling, the more effective I become. I don't have to rise above my emotions to escape my reality. I rise above them so that I can make better decisions about things that were going on in my life. Rising above emotions does not mean to suppress them or act like they are not what they are. It means to not allow them to get the best of you.

Once I confronted my emotions, I was able to rise above them. I had no choice but to go up. I started ridding myself of the vanity.

This journey for me is about being alive and aware of myself in each moment of my life. I had to be honest with myself and forgive myself in order to be myself. I had to accept myself in truth so that I could see where I was traveling to. I began living in the moment. I started listening to my feelings and my emotions and handled them in that moment. I did not leave unsettled emotions and feelings lingering in my mind. I dealt with them then so that I would not create surface level happiness covering unsettled pain.

I'm not interested in living in my shadow. So, I stood up with faith and claimed my light knowing that each destination was elevating me to another height. I found the greatest transportation located within. My mind carried me just like the wind. The higher I became I realized that it's really no end. The journey only stops when you stop believing, when you lose faith or when you lose sight of where you are going.

I'm no longer afraid of the unknown heights. I started listening to my soul and at that point my mind, body, and spirit started working together in harmony. This journey is now fun and full of life. I know now that I can go as high as the heavens above and beyond if that's what I want to do. There are limits. The universe belongs to me too.

So, I would say these words to anyone who is searching for their freedom:

Deal with what is holding you back because it is your time. You deserve to free the slave you have become. Yes, I said slave you have become because when you are not acting in your nature or living your purpose you become a slave to others.

What I would say to those who try to force people into acting like they think they should act or enslave them is this:

Your real problem is with yourself! But do to your internal weakness, mental laziness, and lack of desire to be better; you try to enslave others stealing their energy and light because you have blocked your own. You're so arrogant that you can't even see that you are blind, deaf and dumb because you're clueless to the power that God has placed within you. People like you are the real enemies of God in my eyes because you try to enslave the gifts he put in others! Your real problem is with God, but you can't get to Him so you try to shut him off within your brother or sister. Get your lazy ass up and be who God created you to be and stop being a light snatcher!

What I would share with the members of the Nation is this:

Accepting my own and being myself, is allowing the light that God put in me to shine. Being on the journey to freedom has resurrected me and in that resurrection I'm able to be a better person, a better vessel for God's work. This journey to freedom has aided me in loving myself and finding purpose for life. Now I treat others with that love. I not only say I want for my sister or brother what I want for myself, I say it with meaning and follow it up with actions.

I want us all to be cleaned up, not just from physical abuse, but this journey has cleaned my mind and spirit up. I think the journey would benefit those in the nation because it will help them to find their truth which will allow them to use the truth that God gave them to become a 'saviour' of humanity.

When I did not know my light, I tried to trick myself into thinking that I was shining my real light by saying things like, "I don't smoke, drink, or fornicate."

I had the law, but I did not have the love. I looked every place except within myself, and when I finally went within and started working on myself, I no longer had to say what I don't do. People started loving me for me. By shining my light, others can come out of darkness. All praise is due to Almighty God for depositing a part of Himself within us; and to me that's worth sharing with the world.

What I would say to the Minister who preaches truth is this:

Keep teaching, because even within the misunderstanding of your teaching is understanding. All may not comprehend the love that's in your message, but it is okay because its reaching those who are ready. Your positive, real, genuine, authentic-self is changing the tone of the universe and setting the atmosphere to unchain the minds of the people on a spiritual level. You're needed. You are loved, so never stop awakening the hearts of the people!

Why would anyone want to spend their whole life trying to help someone else live their dreams while they themselves starve spiritually? I had to learn that it was necessary for me to include myself in the process and that by sharing my talents with the world, I was helping the mission. And to my sisters and brothers in the Nation of Islam, if the goal is to strive to love my brother and my sister as I love myself, then I had to start by learning to love myself. If the goal is to strive to improve myself spiritually, morally, mentally, socially, politically and economically for the benefit of myself, my family and my people, then I'm doing that too on my journey to freedom. If the goal is to strive to build businesses, build houses, build hospitals, build factories and enter into international trade for the good of myself, my family and my people, then I'm doing my part in that too by starting a business and working to make that business a success.

I have what the Creator gave me and that is what is needed for me to do my part in the above. I have to start with myself and that is what this journey is all about. So, learning to live truthfully to me is about being and doing me first and foremost. It takes believing in me and having a direct connection with God.

My Aha Moment:

 I'm learning that it's very healing in living truthfully. It takes courage. I'm learning that truthful living is more than something you tell to others. It is a healthy lifestyle. When you're not being honest, you're going against your very existence.

I had to ask myself, "How can you go against the truth of your being, and be well and successful?"

In me learning to live truthfully, I had to start helping my mind, body and soul to heal. I started by being truthful. It has actually helped my blood pressure, and lifted a lot of weight off of me.

Trying to hide my internal tears
running from the pain.
Living inside my fear
but who would of known.
A change was near,
so I switched my gears.
I refocused my thoughts,
'cause there's no truth in the lies I bought.
So I sent them back.
I refuse to accept things like that.
False friendship, false love, a fake image,
disguised as self-love.
Oh but now I see,
my freedom is inside of me.

5
EXPERIENCING LIFE'S MAGIC

Unraveling your gifts,
creating a universal shift,
unleashing your mind,
putting a freeze on time,
and changing life's motion
with the music of your heart.
Every step you take creates beautiful art.
The heavens will sing,
and the worlds will know your name
because of the magic in your soul
unleashing your stories that were never told.
The power is in you...
And, your only duty is to be true.

It seems to me that when I share my gifts, it is taking in life and giving back inspiration to the world. So why should I limit myself to the physical body? Why not be all of me? I'm setting myself free on all levels.

This is about you finding my magic and not apologizing for being me. Everybody may not like the real me and that's okay. Maybe they were not meant for the real me. I'm going to be myself. I'm going to do what makes me happy! I'm going to do what makes my heart sing. I will not spend my precious, beautiful, and unique life sitting around doing what makes others happy and deny myself happiness.

Many times we get living a righteous life mixed up with rituals. Some people feel like if they pray that makes them righteous, or if they attend church or mosque on a regular basis that makes them righteous. Some believe that the so called sinner and unrighteous ones are the ones who don't attend church or mosque meetings.

Prayer alone will not make you righteous. Attending every church or mosque meeting will not make you right-eous. You have to be right to yourself. Treating yourself right starts with being honest with who you are. I am finding the magic in being myself. I realized that I have the

God-given power to influence the universe just by being myself. I'm a part of the whole. To understand that the Creator thought enough of me to allow me to be birthed into the world is magical. I have something to offer this world, and so whenever I start to think unloved and reject-ed, I remember that there is no one else in the world like me and I am loved, and I wouldn't be here if the Creator didn't see me fit to be here in this time.

I started living life in the moment, and I realized that each moment led me to dig deeper into the truth of myself and what I believed to be true about me. Each time I go deeper within, I discovered things that I had no idea was in me. Now that's magical.

We have treasures within us but we don't find our treas-ures when we are busy looking for it in others. I found rubies, diamonds, pearls, and emeralds inside. And each gem within me has a meaning that I am extracting.

I'm a ruby because I have courage.
I'm a diamond because I'm a committed person.
I'm a pearl because of my faith.
I'm an emerald because I'm a very valuable person.

I experience life's magic by overcoming challenges that look impossible. I experience life's magic by bringing my ideas to life. Magic to me happens every time I'm able to bring one of my ideas into existence. Love is magic! Being able to purge your heart and soul, digging deep into the unknown parts of your heart and mind, finding your hidden treasure is magical!

I believe that God has everything in order for me. Everything I need on my journey is already available to me. Not having to worry about what I have or don't have. That's magical. Don't worry about what you have. Being able to trust that I will have everything I need when I need it. That's magical.

Life is not the same for me since I began my journey to freedom. Things like eating healthier are not a hassle for me anymore. I find myself wanting to do it because of my new found purpose in life. I want to live to fulfill my purpose.

I view every day that I'm alive as my time. Every day is my season. I realize that there are just different seasons in my life to manifest different things and parts of myself. But as long as I'm alive, it's my time. So I plan on using my time wisely by walking in my greatness and letting my light shine. And that's a magical feeling!

It's amazing how I started meeting different people at different times that assisted in a particular area. I did not have to try to figure that out, they just began to appear. It seems that life was being brought out of every situation I touched. I realized that life doesn't have to be miserable, it is a gift given to us, and I am determined to receive it with thanksgiving.

Although I started experiencing life's magic, there are times I face challenges, and times I get sad. Sometimes I even feel like giving up, but I don't. I believe that if you live good, good will come to you.

The magic of life looks like happiness and peace of mind. Being able to walk the earth with hardly any worries because you know you already have what you need in life is a magical feeling. Every time I learn something new about myself is a magical moment. Learning, growing and just being is magical.

My Aha Moment:

As I experience the magic of life, I'm learning that nothing is impossible and not only is things not impossible, God made all things achievable. I'm learning to trust my own self and not look for others to create my magic. I'm learning to have faith in the person who God created me to be and as I have faith and look for inner peace I realize it opens up a greater relationship with God. I'm no longer running from the God in me. When I connect with God like that, it's magical! I'm strengthening my relationship with God. This is a direct connection.

I realize now that God is with me and I have a wonderful chance to experience the Saterria that I had been imagining.

Following the beat within my heart,
creating a song from my soul.
Stepping into a new reality,
Allowing my true colors to show.
Letting my mind run free,
No longer am I a slave to the other side of me.

Yes! Yes! Yes! I'm free.
Free to speak my truth,
Free to walk in my faith,
Free from the lies.

So now I look honesty in the face.
No more hidden tears.
I acknowledge that love is real,
And the healer of all pain.
Yes there is sunshine after the rain.
Create your rainbow, and shine in your truth.

...Conclusion, until next time

For every ending there is a beginning. Sometimes there is a fear of new beginnings. On my journey to freedom, which I'm still on, at each turn there has been a new beginning. There has been a lot of letting go. There has been a lot of uncovering. In order for me to continue on this journey that I had been writing to you about, I still have to overcome some fears. I have to give up the fear of being alone. I have to give up being afraid of going even deeper within my own mind, body and soul. I have to be willing to continue to flow.

Looking back, I've come a long way. Do I still have a ways to go? Yes! But as long as I put my complete trust in the Creator victory is mine and because I believe that, I will continue to walk in my faith like a warrior already claiming my win.

I don't know your journey and I don't know your struggle, but I do know that we all face struggles. That is a common denominator. You might even have fears too.

But what I would say to you is this, "Do not allow your fears to keep you from being the person that you were born to be."

I know fear holds me back. So I will take it one day at a time in overcoming them because I want to be free and I do have the courage to live freely in every area of my life. I didn't know me like I know myself now. Each day I learn more and more about who I am.

During this journey I've gained more confidence and accomplished some things that I have wanted to do for a long time. At first, I didn't think I could do it, but I did. I'm so glad that I decided to stay the course. Life can and does get better. But when you are depressed you don't always see things clearly. At one point when I was depressed, I thought of committing suicide. But that is not the answer. And if I had done that, I wouldn't have gotten to this point of where I am now. So, if you are reading this and you are thinking about taking your own life, don't make a final decision based on a temporary situation. It does get better. But you have to believe that. If you need someone to talk to call me, I can do my best to help reassure you that things does get better.

If you need help urgently because you are feeling extremely down, please reach out and talk about it. Don't hesitate to call:

National Suicide Prevention Lifeline
1-800-273-TALK (8255)

You are not alone. It does help to talk about it. It helps to write how you are feeling too.

You see, I needed to free myself from the bondage that I was in. Once I started the process of doing that, things began to get better.

Originally, when I set out to write this book, I had something different in mind. I wasn't trying to tell my story. But God saw something different. Months before writing, *My Journey to Freedom*, I was still trying to control the situation, instead of just letting go and letting God.

I felt the need to control things in my life, but in this case, I realized that I was going to have to just let go. I had to stop controlling every situation and listen to my heart.

My heart said, "Open the Facebook group for women and start right there."

This became the base of the women's group that I wanted to do, and I already had everything I needed in that moment.

In this group, another sister and I teamed up to do a 30-day inspirational movement sharing some of our stories and how we overcame certain events in our lives. We did this so that others who may be going through something similar can find strength in the stories shared.

Although I shared "my story" on Facebook during the 30-day inspirational movement, this book, *My Journey to Freedom* is my testimony. Is it a complete testament of my life? No… But it is the start of the real Saterria stepping out on the platform of life, being and living truthfully.

So, as I conclude this book I also conclude the part of my life where I live through my pain not being real about myself or my feelings. This journey thus far has encouraged me to gather the scattered pieces of my life, forced me to rise above the hurt and pain, inspired me to accept the best part of self, guided me to live truthfully; and now, I'm ready to consistently experience life's magic. I choose to express my true self with no apologies living up to every gift that the Creator deposited in me on… My Journey to Freedom!

About The Author

Saterria Springer Norah, who has been writing and keeping diaries since very young, is a wife and mother who was born and reared in Wilmington, North Carolina in the center of town in a six-family home, which included her mother, father, and three brothers.

She founded the Little Gods Academy Homeschool seven years ago and has had a love for writing, music and teaching for some time, and has kept a diary from childhood to the present.